A Complicated Grief

Anushka Patricia

BookLeaf Publishing

India | USA | UK

Presentation by *BookLeaf Publishing*

Web: www.bookleafpub.com

E-mail: info@bookleafpub.com

ISBN: 9789357449106

First edition 2022

DEDICATION

For all those who have experienced a different
kind of loss

ACKNOWLEDGEMENT

Thank you to those friends who have never shied away from the difficult conversations and have checked in with me even months and years after the initial grief set in. I couldn't have got through the last few years without you. To Mama for letting me talk to you about my childhood even when it was hard for you to hear. To B, for always being there. To M & J for being my home.

Narcissus child

Growing up
You lifted me up
You fought my corner
And taught me to be proud
Of where we had come from
What I wanted to become
You showed me to dream
And how to work hard

But growing up
You also kept me down
When I spoke my mind
You were quiet for months
What I knew to be truths
You told me were lies
When I loved another
I saw your fire

Growing up
You were rarely around
You said it was for us
But it was also for name
I wish you had cared less
About accolades and fame
Our lives were separate
Already estranged

Growing up
I was anchored adrift
I was your all in one moment
Nothing the next
After so long
I now realise the cost
Of what I have gained
But also what has been lost

Divorce

After decades together,
she finds her confidence,
her courage to go.
She tells him its over,
she's not coming home.

He thinks it will pass,
as it's done
so many times before.
But then it dawns: she's gone,
she's no longer his to own.

She struggles at first,
her life without him
unknown.
The pull to go back
like a bird flying home.

He doesn't understand
what was different
this time.
How could this happen
to a man of his kind?

She starts to build a life.
Freedom.
The first she has known.
She misses him deeply
but knows she must roam.

He blames all he can,
but never
doubts himself.
He calls all their friends
to spin his own web.

She hears his tales
of her deceit
from far and from wide.
She lets him hold court
but questions his mind.

He cannot let go.
He wants
to rule on all sides.
But he is all alone now,
just him and his pride.

A love dismantled.
Two separate lives
have begun.
A family brought down
to a kingdom of one.

Only child syndrome

5

They don't tell you how it
Feels to be the
Third person
In a family being
Divided into two

It is a mutilation

Strangers

Just like that we became
Strangers
Born of you but our
Lives apart
Divorce for you shouldn't mean
Divorce for us
I am still
Your daughter
However much it hurts

Flowers without a vase

You ask me to forgive you
Like I used to
When I was a girl

But it's too late
You have taken away a part of us
That cannot be returned

You say I'm not your child
I feel like flowers
Without a vase

I feel lost
And just helpless
But want to survive in this world

And so I fill the void
With work
Like you taught me

Emotional amputation

Some people ask
How you draw that line
Cut a person you love
Out of your life
I say the same way that
Sometimes we
Cut off an arm
To save the rest of the body
The nerves are still there
You can feel it move
You can feel its loss
But you had to do it

Lines

Lines in front of her
Green pen
Red pen
A daughter's life
In full flow-

Lines in front of him
This pill
That pill
A father's life
All but gone-

That day

The chapters of my life
Now only divide into
Before and
After
That Day
Or did I start a new book

Undead

The call came
It said you were almost dead
I should sit down
It was not in my head

You had done this to yourself
You had wanted the end
You had meant me to feel bad
Is what the letters said
Six days you had lain there
Alone in your bed
Before they rescued you
To salvage what was left

As the doctor recounted
I lost all sense of self
My mind was above
The body it dwelt
Then a noise left my mouth
Like flesh being sliced
The sound still haunts me
Like the ghost of that night

Weeks asleep
Hope, a vanishing sun
I mourned for your life
But also our story un-done
As guilt took hold
More powerful than the sea
A realisation we would never mend
The break in our tree

I wished you peace
To end the war you had begun
An acceptance then
Of the songs un-sung
Then suddenly you awoke
Like a vampire reborn
Now you are alive
But I can't un-mourn

Not my story

The more I tell
My story
Your story
Our story
The more it feels
Like it happened to
Someone else

Guilt

Is it wrong
That I felt relief
When I thought you were dead

Is it wrong
That I ignored the pain
And went to work the next day

Is it wrong
That I felt guilt
But still can't let myself come near

Is it wrong
That I felt shame
About losing a parent that way

Is it wrong
That I was angry
When you denied what you had done

Is it wrong
That I felt hurt
When I knew you were hurting worse

Is it wrong
That I felt fear
When I knew you had survived

Is it wrong
That I felt stronger
When I put myself first

Everything is different

I feel different somehow,
Like I've opened my eyes
To see the world for the first time.
I can't un-see it
Because the world is different now
And so am I.

I'm screaming at the friends
Who knew me so well.
To explain what I've seen.
But they can't understand me
Because they are different now
And so am I.

I get back to work,
The place where I feel safe,
To distract me from what I've seen.
But it doesn't have the same meaning
Because it's different now
And so am I.

I reach for those who were with me,
Who saw it for themselves..
I beg for shared recollection
But their eyes saw it differently.

Because they are different now
And so am I.

17

The fear

It came out of nowhere
A stab in the dark
A sting under the sheets
Sand sinking below my feet
Now out of nowhere
Fear-
Of the dark
Of my dreams
Of walking ahead

Disenfranchised

There isn't a card
For this kind of loss
Which can make it feel so
Unseen
Unwarranted
Unreal

Then how come
This pain
Feels more true than any
Good luck
Congratulations
Thank you

Life is shorter

It's hard to explain
but grief
has made life
shorter somehow.
More unpredictable.
More precious.
Less tolerant.
There's less time now.

For the large parties,
where you speak to everyone,
but really
feel alone.
For the old friends
in your phonebook
you know you've
outgrown.

For the meaningless and
the mundane.
For the empty conversations
without soul.
For those who deny all imperfection
in the need
to keep things
whole.

For the relentless emails,
day and night.
For the stress and
the greys.
For only seeing a
slight of this earth
when the whole world
awaits.

For going through the motions,
just sitting on
the conveyer belt
of life.
For not carving out
your own identity,
for fear of difference
if you try.

Adjustment

What happened
Has changed me
Fundamentally
Broke me
Repeatedly
Nothing fits anymore
But maybe
It never fit
Perhaps
It never understood me
Or I never let it know me
Fully
If it had
It would have made me feel at ease
Grown with me
Gradually
This is my chance
Unexpectedly
To reposition
To liberate
To be more me

The race

I have never understood why
Everyone is in such a rush
To win the race
Head down
First kiss
First love
Sex
Get a job
Get a mortgage
Get married
Have babies
Don't they know
That there are many more laps
That there are other races
That you have to pace
Yourself

Old/young

Childish woman
Playful wife
Silly friend
Others age and
Expect you to grow up
But is it any wonder you are
Stuck
In a childhood you lost to
Being their old soldier
You were the sensible toddler
The grown up child
The mature princess

Integrity's dilemma

25

If I wear what I want to wear
Where it isn't the worn thing
Will I be worn down
If I do what I want to do
Where it isn't the done thing
Will I come undone
If I say what I want to say
Where it isn't to the said thing
Will I be heard
If I believe what I want to believe
Where people don't believe
Will hope leave me
If I love who I want to love
Where it isn't seen as love
Will I feel unloved
If I am who I want to be
But I stand alone
Will they see me
Or will they look away

Ladies first

First I was a little girl
in an ocean of little boys,
breaking down barriers
as the first of my kind.
I was queuing for my milk
when 'Ladies first!' they cried,
so I hopped, skipped and jumped my way
straight to the front of the line.
Oblivious to the misogyny
behind what they had said,
but also empowered never to allow
The men to get ahead.

Then I was a little brown girl
in a sea of white.
I was made to feel welcome
but I knew I didn't belong.
It's hard not to notice
that you're the odd one out,
so I started to hide my heritage
just to get along.
I didn't realise then
that I would regret washing out
the thing that made me different,
that should have made me proud.

When I became a brown girl
in a motley crew,
they said I was too brown
but then not brown enough.
So I focused on my work,
kept my identity tightly wrapped,
aimed to break the mould
To fit into every rough.
In the middle of the tribes,
neither here nor there.
Sacrificing ancestral substance
to survive childhood's glare.

Then I became a brown woman
in a melting pot.
Without even realising,
I was reverting to type.
As I saw more inequality:
I recognised my worth,
I began to value my difference,
my confidence grew ripe.
My voice got louder,
more impatient with this world,
more driven to challenge injustice and
Not to follow the herd.

Finally a brown feminist
In a, supposedly, tolerant world,
I can see the inequity around me,
the endless work to be done.
I thank the little girl in the queue
who never stood back;
the brown woman who finally decided
not to hide, pretend or run.
To the diversity in my life that has often made me
question where I belong:
I now thank you for giving me the courage
to stand up, to be strong.

Home

When home became hard
The fights too loud
The silence too much
I found quiet in books
Solace in fantasy
And comfort in achievement
I learnt I was sad
But success could make me happy

When success became hard
The energy too high
The inequality too tiring
I found the quiet in us
Solace in nature
And comfort in you
I learnt I had choices
That being home could make me happy